ARROW OF TIME

And Other Poems of Anonymity and Dissolution

CHEW LAWRENCE

PARTRIDGE

A Penguin Random House Company

To order additional copies of this book, contact
Toll Free 800 101 2657 (Singapore)
Toll Free 1 800 81 7340 (Malaysia)
orders.singapore@partridgepublishing.com

www.partridgepublishing.com/singapore

Contents

For my wife Adeline

and our boys

Jonathan and Joshua

Foreword

Chew would disclaim that his first collection is a body of metaphysical poetry, yet his poems are metaphysical in that they pose questions about the fundamental nature of reality and posits the poet's tentative answers concerning it.

Unlike the metaphysical poets of the 17th century such as John Donne and George Herbert who looked to God as Ultimate Reality, the poet disavows any notion of Deity. To him, God is not the personal divine being of believers, but a "Poet of Creation" who "teaches us the songs of ascension that lifts forth the universe". This "Poet of Creation" in turn is the poet's creation - a metaphor. That he slips into this metaphor is revealing – both of the poet and our distinctly human proclivity to awe and wonder.

Nonetheless his "relationship" with a non-existent God is one of mock reverence. This is evident in the lines where he plays upon the declaration of Christ: "Before Father Abraham was, I am" and cheekily inserts: "Amoeba in water, ape-man on land: I devolve as I evolve into degenerate man" who kills "with consummate ease, rape and mutilate where I please." Written in the first person, the amoebic persona celebrates its self-interested fight for its survival:

A micro-byte of a smudge;
I ooze in, I ooze out sludge.
Light effloresces on my skin;
I glow into a glob of gelatin.

I severally divide and multiply,
I slit-split into twos; in zillions I ply

The primordial slime: I suck
And suckle on uncultured muck.

Murky years pass, late than soon,
I gorge me into 'protozoon'.
I grow filaments; I roundly swim
And feed on fellows 'protozim'.

Where then do humans stand in Chew's godless universe, one in which *'Dreams and miracles come together, Entropically, fall apart together?'* Perhaps this verse in *Somewhere Somewhen* hints to our place in the cosmic context:

And somewhere at all moments,
A newborn babe is crying
As somewhere else that moment,
Some babe's mother is dying.

The tender lyricism of the lines does not diminish our unique penchant to seek self-authentication and meaning; but rather gently counsels a sense of proportion in our reaction to suffering when seen from a universal perspective.

To read his poems is to be invited into the swirling vortex of quantum physics, philosophy, evolutionary biology and personal biography. They do not make an easy read, but engaging with them is not only a stimulating intellectual exercise, it may lead the reader to ponder the nature of the universe and our place in it. In these poems, you meet the defiance of modern man, stripped of the easy consolations of God, conversing with silent space:

I *shall like to live my life as a Promethean poem*
And steal to earth God's most sacred fire from heaven!

By stealing fire from God, Chew shares the light he lives by with his readers, even as he mocks the grandiosity of his own endeavor.

> *Yes, I shall like to live free as a poem of fired art!*
> *But no, old fiends and friends, this tired old heart*
> *Is but one tiresome old fart! One highfalutin cretin*
> *And one low sorry fellow of creation and damnation;*
> *Prometheus-fired poem I am not but lout and tout:*
> *Where my poetry soars, it eats my heart inside out!*

Chew refers to his anthology as poems of anonymity and dissolution. In *Arrow of Time*, the title poem of this anthology, he notes that *All I denominate as dollar* time will *decimate as dime*. And in *Nights with no Glimmer of Moon*, he remembers in hard times the kindness of an unknown woman as 'anonymity'.

> *The years of unpunctuated poverty*
> *Broke into dawns with a small glimmer of moon*
> *In which I remember only her anonymity*
>
> *And like one now disabused*
> *Of the terrifying clutches of a cataplectic dream*
> *I gratefully remember naught else*

Nor does Chew believe in an afterlife but in its dissolution: In *A Dream of Being in a Trefoil Tunnel*, he writes of a dream in which the '*subliminal meets the sublime*' but concludes:

> *Ignoramus et ignorabimus!* I wake but know not
> If death be a cingulated sleep so dark and deep
> One dreams not of waking but of staying asleep!

If you have an ear for the lyrical and yet love to probe mysteries and bust myths, you will love Chew's poems. The lyricism ranges from the personal to the cosmic. He does not pull his punches yet remarkably, delivers them in songs – right from the first to the last poem in this anthology.

Jeffery Lee
(Singapore poet)

Arrow of Time

Swift entropic arrow of time,
You illicit my poetic freedom!
You vex me inside-out of rhythm,
Outside-in of rhyme;

You irreversible debacle
And thermodynamic oracle,
Too late I learn: in my present
Wanes a future crescent!

How like an even sun I set;
How, sliver of moon, I wane;
Loafer poet, how shall I not regret
The poems I didn't beget?

Sharp-cutting quarrel of time!
You go for the jugular;
All I denominate as dollar
You decimate as dime.

Lawrence Chew
20 April 2014

Notes for **Arrow of Time**

The arrow of time is a 'thermodynamic' arrow in that it obeys the laws governing the nature of heat, the two most notable being that entropy or disorder in an isolated system never decreases with time, and heat always moves from a hot to a cold place. The poet laments to himself the swift passage of time and its debilitating effects on all human endeavors, not least his poetic endeavors.

Entropic: of entropy or disorder that grows with time

Illicit: to disapprove of; to outlaw

Vex: cause annoyance

Debacle: sudden or ludicrous failure; fiasco

Thermodynamic: of the dynamics or flow of heat

Loafer poet: the poet addresses himself

Quarrel: a pun, a 'quarrel' is both a dispute and the head of an arrow

Jugular: of, relating to, or located in the region of the neck or throat.

Denominate: to assign value in terms of a monetary unit

Decimate: to destroy a part of

Dollar; dime: metaphorical allusion to the futility of all endeavors and material acquisition

An Atheist's Portraiture of God as the Poet of Creation

In the great dark void before He made our universe,
God was primordially drunk on poetry and verse;
Poesy sublimely crowned His high and haloed head
As subliminally, He poeticized the decrees He made.

In that last timeless even, before the first-born morn,
He created chaos and the great cold void without form:
For quite forgot He, darkness was conceptualized first
To conceive, mid-wife, and deliver forth the universe

For afore He uttered the first fiat, 'Let there be light,'
And separated He the dark ebony void from the bright,
White light, decrees He, symbolizes Hope and Right,
Ebony black, decrees He, symbolizes Evil and Blight.

He painterly personifies as a bridegroom the rising sun,
Who, coming out of his tent, joyously makes ready to run
His light-long race: yea, the princes of the night sky dim
Their faces; they bow out as one constellated sky before him.

The moon He womanizes as one who duly keeps
The Sabbaths and holy months; at one vesper, sleeps
She not but keeps her wholesome eye over the forlorn
House of Israel in the embattled valley of Ajalon.

O Poet-God, anoint us again with psalms of poetry and verse,
Teach us the songs of ascension that lift forth the universe;
Lift the curse; let Earth bring forth again the fats of the land
As in the days when innocent God hearkens to the voice of man!

O Painter of proses, in what new valleys and secret Eden
Walk you now with fig-less Eve and Adam at even?
In what hidden spheres, sing you now your new verses,
In what new gardens light years away, in what new universes?

Lawrence Chew
18 December 2012

Notes for **An Atheist's Portraiture of God as the Poet of Creation**

In a metaphorical manner of speaking, the poem paints a portrait of God as a master painter and poet hard at work during creation. Various criticism of divine creation is interspersed in between the lavish praises for God.

Primordially: being original or happening first in sequence of time
Poesy: Poetry
Sublimely: of a noble or majestic nature
Haloed: encircled with light about the head
Subliminally: being below the threshold of consciousness
Poetized: made into poetry
Even: evening
Conceptualized, conceive, mid-wife and deliver: metaphor associated with birth
Ebony: black
Painterly: like a painter or artist
Personifies: describes as a person
Womanizes: depicts as a woman
Vesper: evening
Ajalon: see Joshua 10:12 - 14
Songs of ascension: psalms or 'songs of degrees' (sung as devout Jews ascend the hills of Jerusalem)

Before Abraham was I am

(A Versification of the Evoluted Past in the Convoluted Present Tense)

Once upon a billion aeons ago,
When mucks are gene pools of protozoa;
Long before Ape is the forebear of Abraham
And amoeba the forebear of ape-man, I am...

A micro-byte of a smudge;
I ooze in, I ooze out sludge.
Light effloresces on my skin;
I glow into a glob of gelatin.

I severally divide and multiply,
I slit-split into twos; in zillions I ply
The primordial slime: I suck
And suckle on uncultured muck.

Murky years pass, late than soon,
I gorge me into 'protozoon'.
I grow filaments; I roundly swim
And feed on fellows 'protozim'.

Generations pass in the slow blink
Of an ill-formed eye; I slither-slink,
Grow gill-lungs in sun-soaked brine,
And breathe air of rain-soaked shine.

My androgynous brothers take roots on land,
My amorphous sisters lay eggs in twigs and sand:

Though Nature is select,
I elect to walk erect -

I stride roughshod on two-footed-falls,
Legs gangly astride two corpulent balls;
Thighs astraddle a cock of insolent stub,
I dangle erect an alpha-male-size club.

I grow a brain coconut size
I eat, sleep and strategize;
I kill with consummate ease,
Rape and mutilate where I please.

I harem and fornicate;
I wage wars and dominate;
The little 'i am that i am' of the earth,
I am the least that is the first.

O First Cause and God of Abraham,
Before Father Abraham was, I am
Amoeba in water, ape-man on land:
I devolve as I evolve into degenerate man.

Lawrence S.T. Chew
22. 12. 2012

Notes for **Before Abraham was I am**

This poem pokes fun at the creationist theory. The title is taken from John 8: 48 - 58.

Protozoa: microscopic organisms

Amoeba: a subclass of protozoa

Micro-byte: small bit of information (intended as a metaphor)

Effloresce: to bloom, flower

Glob of gelatin: small or tiny ball of gel-like substance

Primordial: original; happening first in sequence of time

Protozoon: same as protozoa

Protozim: 'Hebrew' for protozoa (specially coined to rhyme with 'swim'; this poetic license is justified by the fact that Abraham is a Jew)

Androgynous: producing only male offspring

Amorphous: lacking definite form or shape

Corpulent balls: excessively fat testes

Cock of insolent stub: penis with an arrogant swagger

Alpha-male-size club: large penis of a leading male

The little i am that i am: allusion to Exodus 3:14

I am the first that am the last: allusion to Revelation 22:13

First Cause: a term of address that acknowledges God as the creator of the universe

A Dream of Being in a Trefoil Tunnel

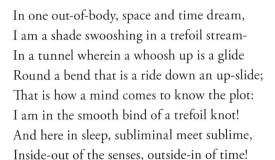

In one out-of-body, space and time dream,
I am a shade swooshing in a trefoil stream-
In a tunnel wherein a whoosh up is a glide
Round a bend that is a ride down an up-slide;
That is how a mind comes to know the plot:
I am in the smooth bind of a trefoil knot!
And here in sleep, subliminal meet sublime,
Inside-out of the senses, outside-in of time!

I go pass the upturns of days riding a light-beam,
I go pass the downturns of nights at time-zero;
Light and shadow flee as one intermittent stream
At vaporeal velocities the mass of radii sub-zero;
And ignoramuses the hulk of hippopotamuses,
And savants the brain of many polycephaluses,
Atheists, Quakers, agnostics and whatnots, alike
Swoosh as zeros of nothing in the half-light.

Ignoramus et ignorabimus! I wake but know not
If death be a cingulated sleep so dark and deep
One dreams not of waking but of staying asleep!

Lawrence Chew
14 Sep 2103

Notes for **A Dream of Being in a Trefoil Tunnel**

This 'surreal' poem is a refutation of out-of-body near-death experiences (NDE). Often, an individual with such an experience declares finding himself in a tunnel of light before finally meeting a mysterious figure (Jesus or some such persons) who then tells him to return to his body. The persona (or *voice*) in this poem does not claim to have a near-death experience; he merely has a dream in which he leaves his body and finds himself in a tunnel in the shape of a trefoil knot. The trefoil knot, pictured here, is the symbol for infinity:

To refute out-of-body experiences, the poet counterchecks superstitions against scientific knowledge. For instant, the NDE individual often reports walking at a nominal pace in the tunnel. This, the poet counters, cannot be correct. A departed soul travels at the speed of light (if not faster) because it has no mass. In deed, if a soul could pass through solids, it has less mass than a photon (particle of light). It should therefore be superluminal! The first verse employs sibilants (words with the s sounds) for creating onomatopoeic effects associated with swift movement and sleep: e.g. whoosh, swoosh, sleep, sublime, subliminal etc. In the imagined trefoil tunnel, the 'soul' moves at the speed of light – which to the poet's best of knowledge has never before being reported. Hence, the poet claims, the individual cannot claim to have an out-of-body experience. What he experiences is hallucination in which he loses all sense of speed and dimensions and in which the subliminal meets the sublime! The refutation is further pursued in the second verse: the individual should meet the shades (i.e. spirits or ghosts) of all people of all sizes, professions and beliefs – all travelling at the speed of light.

Ignoramuses: unintelligent people

Savants: very intelligent people

Polycephaluses: many headed persons (poetic license employed)

Ignoramus et ignorabimus: Latin for 'I do not know and shall not know'

Cingulated: bound within a *cingulum*, medical term for a girdle-like structure

Nights with No Glimmer of Moon

(An Unpunctuated Poem)

Nights with no glimmer of moon
In your half-silvered mirror
Anonymity silhouettes fading memories

Ages ago I was a child trapped
In the nightmare clutches of scorn and penury
And playmates I had but few

I half-remember of an early evening
A short play-reach of a half-lit house
The anonymous mother of an anonymous friend

Called out hello and gave
As would Mother Teresa to an impoverished boy
A little something of a treat to eat

My rat eyes gleamed
A chocolate-coated nut it was she gave me
My first taste of chocolate

The years of unpunctuated poverty
Broke into dawns with a small glimmer of moon
In which I remember only her anonymity

And like one now disabused
Of the terrifying clutches of a cataplectic dream
I gratefully remember naught else

Lawrence Chew
7 February 2014

Notes for **Nights with no Glimmer of Moon**

A poem based on the poet's childhood experience.

Half-silvered mirror: mirror that reflects light unevenly or in different directions

Anonymity: the condition of being unknown

Silhouettes: the dark shape and outline of someone or something

Penury: extreme poverty

Unpunctuated: metaphor for 'without pause'

Disabused: set free of

Cataplectic: of cataplexy or sleep paralysis in which the victim in his dream feels the terror of being unable to waken

A Song of Willy-nilly Nill and Will

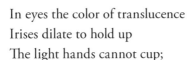

In eyes the color of translucence
Irises dilate to hold up
The light hands cannot cup;

In minds the color of efflorescence
Cool heads may not prevail,
Hot heads may not fail;

But in mindsets the color of prison walks
Thoughts clog dead-end street,
Clatter on tombstone feet;

And most, in hearts the color of talks
Spirit wields wills,
Flesh, willy-nilly, nills.

From wombs we come willy-nilly will
Whence from ripe to rot, we rot and rot;
So to tombs we go willy-nilly nill.

Lawrence Chew
23 February 2014

Notes for **A Song of Willy-nilly Nill and Will**

There are personal traits and events that we can or cannot control. How much one can do in given circumstances depends most on one's personality. Our birth and death are two events entirely beyond our control.

Translucence: the quality of allowing light to pass or diffuse through

Irises: the membrane behind the cornea of the eyes

Efflorescence: in a state of bloom

Prevail: triumph over

Mindset: established set of altitudes held by a person

Prison walks: yard where prisoners walk in circles

Thoughts: these are personified as prisoners

Clog: cause a bottleneck

Clatter: dull repetitive sound

Willy-nilly: haphazardly; in a careless and unplanned way

Nills: has no will or wish to

An Aqueous Dream

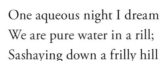

One aqueous night I dream
We are pure water in a rill;
Sashaying down a frilly hill
We sinuate in one stream.

In a lowly bed of translucent
Sand, the moon's up crescent
Runneth over; we fill her up
That fulfils us in her cup;

Dark trees quiver our desires,
White stars mirror our fires;
In amorous and amoral light
We procreate the night.

We seek to rouse but too far
Besotted in our night's begetting
We behold Venus - a betoken star
Neither rising nor setting.

Lawrence Chew
22 April 2014

Notes for **An Aqueous Dream**

This poem employs both onomatopoeic and kinetic effects: it invokes the sound and motion of water and the sound of sleep through the soothing use of sibilants (words carrying an s sound).

Aqueous: of or like water

Sashaying: flowing with a swaying motion

Frilly: adorned with curves

Sinuate: bend or curve; wind in and out

Translucent: of matter that allows some light to pass through

Runneth over (archaic): have more than is desired

Amoral: neither moral nor immoral

Amorous: of or relating to love

Besotted: deeply infatuated; drunk or intoxicated

Begetting: act of procreating

Betoken: be a sign or portend of (unending love)

The Moon and I Sleep-walking

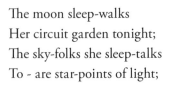

The moon sleep-walks
Her circuit garden tonight;
The sky-folks she sleep-talks
To - are star-points of light;

She sleepwalks alone; above
Considering whom to love;
Her ardent light falls far
Her gentle gaze falls near;

About her sphere a little star
Attenuates in the rear;
Sweet one I don't dare
Dream would love me!

Your ardent gaze falls far
Your gentle eyes fall near;
About you like a little star
I attenuate in the rear.

Lawrence Chew
16 April 2014

Notes for **The Moon and I Sleep-walking**

Circuit: circular route taken by the moon

Garden: metaphor for sky or heaven

Ardent: very enthusiastic or passionate

Attenuate: to weaken or reduce in force, intensity, effect, quantity, or value

A Promethean Poem

I shall like to live my life as a Promethean poem
And steal to earth God's most sacred fire from heaven!
Which prosody, a psalm of echoes in efflorescence;
Which beauty, its raison d'être, the extant of essence;
Which truth, made triune in Pathos, Ethos and Logos,
Lead not the soul up the precipitous brinks of bathos.

I shall like my poem, like unbounded night skies,
Turn long cartwheels across a heaven of seeing eyes
With nary a bolt, nut or hub at its center centrifugal;
With nary an arc or far-off edge at its rim centripetal;
No axle cranks its far-flung revolving eyes of night;
No spokes pent prisoner its far-off pinpoints of light!

Yes, I shall like to live free as a poem of fired art!
But no, old fiends and friends, this tired old heart
Is but one tiresome old fart! One highfalutin cretin
And one low sorry fellow of creation and damnation;
Prometheus-fired poem I am not but lout and tout:
Where my poetry soars, it eats my heart inside out!

Lawrence Chew
7 Sep 2013

Notes for **A Promethean Poem**

In Greek mythology, the titan Prometheus stole fire from heaven, taught its use to man and for this unforgiveable transgression, was eternally bound by Zeus to a rock inside the volcano Mt Edna where daily, Zeus' pet eagle would tear and eat out his liver (believed to be the seat of emotion but referred to as 'heart' in the above poem), which would then regenerate itself by the next morning, only to be torn out and eaten again. Ethos, Pathos and Logos (Credibility, Emotion and Logic) are the 3 Aristotelian modes of persuasion, of which video presentations are available on YouTube.

The poem employs onomatopoeic and kinetic effects. Verse 1 reverberates with echoes; its key phrase is 'echoes in efflorescence'. The verse reverberates with echoes created by the use of alliterations (words beginning with the same letter or sound) and internal and end rhymes. In Verse 2, subject to the physical laws of nature, the poet is Prometheus unbound. Kinetic images are emphasized. Verse 3 reveals the poet's introspective nature: he notes and regrets his failings. Above all, he notes too that introspective poetry is like the eagle that torments Prometheus.

Cogito Ergo Sum

For God and mortals' sake,
Speak no more of *Cogito ergo sum*–
Nor think what I think I become
Nor what form I think I take.

The mind is indivisibly amorphous!
It has no visible or indivisible form;
To invisible thought it is analogous;
Anonymity is its nominal norm.

Like immortals, it covertly goes
Where no mortals dare may go;
Like mortals, it goes on tiptoes
Where fear makes it tremble so!

Go then, filthy, feeble mind!
Know that penitentially evil is the sham
In thinking so beatifically blind,
'I think therefore I am'.

Lawrence Chew
19 March 2014

Notes for **Cogito Ergo Sum**

'Cogito Ergo Sum' (Latin for 'I think therefore I am') is the philosophical statement by which Rene Descartes attempts to prove his existence. The poet has great admiration for the statement but cannot resist the temptation to make light of it. In this poem, he wonders if the 'Cogito' (as the statement is sometimes abbreviated) is more applicable to the 'I' that is the human body or to the 'I' that is the 'mind'. In particular, he is critical of all attempts to debase the Cogito by associating human existence with all notions of the divine and the afterlife.

Cogito Ergo Sum: Latin for I think therefore I am

Amorphous: shapeless; lacking definite form

Analogous: similar to or alike

Anonymity: state of being unknown

Norm: a standard regarded as typical

Nominal: in name only

Covertly: secretly

Penitentially: expressing penitence

Sham: deception passed off as being true

Beatifically: of blessedness

Penitentially evil: oxymoron

Beatifically blind: oxymoron

Déjà vu as Poetry in a Klein-Bottle Universe

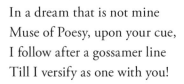

In a dream that is not mine
Muse of Poesy, upon your cue,
I follow after a gossamer line
Till I versify as one with you!

In your Mobius-looped universe
Space regresses as time in reverse;
We versify lost dreams as we glide
Up and down an inverted slide!

Seamless loop of déjà vu universe
In a wine-warmed Klein bottle!
In you, a speck of poetry is a mottle
Regressing forward in reverse!

Come Muse, in dreams déjà vu
Let me nakedly die fulfilling you!
Smother me in your bottle of time,
Sex me up in rhythm and rhyme.

Lawrence Chew
1 May 2014

Notes for **Déjà vu as Poetry in a Klein-Bottle Universe**

In this 'surreal poem', the poet invokes his Muse. He imagines the universe as one Klein bottle – in which 'Space regresses as time in reverse'. The reversal brings to the poet's mind the imagined concept of déjà vu, the perception that a current experience is one that has occurred before in either another place or time or both. For a better grasp of the poem, readers may like to Google 'Klein bottle' and 'Mobius strip'. In 1882, the mathematician Felix Klein imagined sewing together two Mobius strips into a one-sided bottle such that its inside is its outside! Since then, mathematicians have imagined various forms of the Klein bottle, none of which may exist except in a universe with a fourth dimension.

Muse of Poesy: the poet invokes the aid of his muse

Cue: prompting

Gossamer line: a delicate thread-like line (of poetry?)

Kinky: knotty

Speck/mottle: a small spot; tiny amount

Regressing: going backward

Reverse: go backward

Déjà vu: the sensation one has of a situation that had occurred before

Happy Pig: Unhappy Man

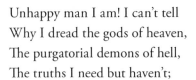

Unhappy man I am! I can't tell
Why I dread the gods of heaven,
The purgatorial demons of hell,
The truths I need but haven't;

Happy pig in a philosopher wig!
Apprentice me earnest and true –
Which to embrace, which to rue,
Unhappy man or happy pig?

'Sad Socrates,' the hog retorts
In tacit snores and tactics snorts -
'Be you wise or cometh short -
No gods kill us for their sport;

Live life as one happy pig
Die death as one happy man;
Only imagined gods wear wig;
Who fears no gods happy am!

Get a life! Live or die your tale,
Stop chasing your airy-fairy tail!
Life and death duly go the round;
Entrance is exit come around.

Lawrence Chew
27 April 2014

Notes for **Happy Pig; Unhappy Man**

This poem is a satirical 'take' on an age-old debate. Over two millennia ago, Socrates asserted that 'The unexamined life is not worth living' and purportedly, asked if it was better to be a happy pig or an unhappy man. The 19 century philosopher John Stuart Mills rephrased the debate thus: "It is better to be a human being dissatisfied than a pig satisfied; better to be Socrates dissatisfied than a fool satisfied. And if the fool, or the pig, is of a different opinion, it is because they only know their own side of the question. The other party to the comparison knows both sides." In the poem, the second persona takes on the role of the 'other party'. It is ironic that he is a 'happy pig in a philosopher's wig'- whether literally or metaphorically is left to the reader's judgment but the pig offers an 'other party' answer worth pondering. Wigs were once fashionable in the upper strata of European society. A man with the pretentious ambitions of mounting the social ladder was called a 'pig in a wig'.

Entrance: metaphor for birth

Exit: metaphor for death

Dog-God Palindrome (What a Howl!)

If a dog were to worship a Dog-God
How would it go? Bow-wow,
Roll over, bark, snap or howl,
As would any dog?

Will it troop or droop its tail,
Flail, fawn, whimper or wail?
Piteously or piously at the moon
Bay plaintively night or noon?

Will the Dog-God be a he-dog or a bitch;
Spotted, russet, white, or black as pitch?
Mongrel, mastiff, Rottweiler or Doberman,
Or the spitting image of man or woman?

As tour de force, will G-o-d and d-o-g
Spell 'God' as 'D-o-g' or 'dog' as 'g-o-d';
Would the twitchy itch to palindrome
Bring on Tourette's syndrome?

Will the God of dogs be called 'Dog-God'
Or will He plainly be called 'God-Dog'?
And will the double-trouble palindrome
Trouble-double Tourette's prodrome?

And when a good or nerdy dog died
How would it be sainted or beatified?

Sirius, Polaris, Procyon or Nerd
Or just plain Saint Bernard?

Lawrence Chew
25 March 2014

Notes on **Dog-God Palindrome**

This is a satirical poem that pokes fun at the need for God. Implicitly, if animals do not have gods, why should we humans need one? A palindrome is a word or phrase spelled the same way forward or backward.

Dog-God: a palindrome

Palindrome: word or phrase that spells the same forward or backward

Troop: parade as a flag

Plaintively: mournfully

Russet: red-brown (of fur)

Tour de force: a feat of great virtuosity

Tourette's syndrome: neurological disorder characterized by multiple facial and body twitching, grunts, dog-like barks, shouts of obscenities and scratching of private parts.

Prodrome: an early symptom indicating the onset of an attack or a disease.

Sirius, Procyon: names of stars or constellations. Sirius (the brightest star in the night sky) is a star of the Sirius constellation – this constellation is Orion's hunting dog. Polaris is the 'north star' and along with Procyon (the brightest in the constellation), are stars in the constellation Canis Minor (also known as Little Dog).

St. Bernard: a breed of very large working dog made famous by tales of alpine rescues.

Horse and Cart

Did wise men from the Buddhist east
Worship the child Jesus as *messiah*?
If so, may not fungible god or fungi yeast
Raise dough over the same fire?

Was it reincarnated *lama* or *messiah*
The Magi come thus far to do homage?
And the heathen kindle in Christ a desire
To free men from hell's appointed bondage?

A horse may draw a cart
But no cart a horse;
One may not seek to divorce
The head from the heart!

Suppose the head is the horse;
Suppose the heart is the cart;
Let the head in scientific discourse
Husband the wifely heart.

Let the horse as the p antecedent
Draw the cart as the q consequent;
In discourse, mind your Ps and Qs;
And give the devil his dues.

In fair words say your pieces,
Skew not truth or recue;

Just mind you your pleases;
Say you your thank yous.

Lawrence Chew
6 May 2014

Notes for Horse and Cart

When a Dalai Lama (or some other godly lama) dies, Tibetan set out in search of his reincarnated soul. It is conceivable that the magi who worshipped the babe Jesus were such Buddhist monks. Tibetan lore and Buddhist scriptures assert that Jesus trained as a monk in India and Tibet before returning to Israel where he was later crucified. Following his resuscitation, he returned to India and Tibet where he is thought to have lived out his remaining years. Buddhists and Christians alike, note that their beliefs are similarly pacific and non-violent in nature. One common saying in the two religions is 'Do unto others what you will have others do undo you.'

Buddhist: of Buddha's teaching (considered by Christians as heathen beliefs)

East: the magi were possibly from India or present day Tibet.

Lama: devout Buddhist leader

Messiah: anticipated savior of the world; the word's italicization emphasizes the poet's doubt that the wise men knew Jesus was God's anointed Messiah.

Dough: flour kneaded with water (veiled allusion to Christ's resurrection)

Fungible: interchangeable

Fungal: of fungi

Divorce/The head from the heart: reason and sentiments should not be divorced from one another

Messiah: a savior chosen or approved by God

Hell's appointed bondage: damnation in hell

Skew: make crooked

Recuse: reject

Verses 5 and 6:

1. The horse drawing the cart analogy (first mentioned in verse 2) is **likened** to a 'if p therefore q argument';

2. The horse is the antecedent part (represented by the letter p) and the cart is the consequent part (represented by the letter q);

3. To assert 'p therefore q' is a valid argument: this is known as asserting the consequent.

4. However, to assert 'q therefore p' is a fallacy i.e. an invalid argument. This fallacy is known as 'denying the antecedent'.

5. In like manner, metaphorically, it is valid to assert that a horse (p) may pull a cart but a fallacy to assert that a cart (q) may pull a horse.

6. Likewise, in verses 1 and 2, the poem is asserting that it is NOT because the babe Jesus is the Christ or messiah that that the magi (wise men) sought him out; rather, it is because the child was visited by the magi that he sought to become the Christ. This is hinted at by the analogy that one may contend that leavened bread which is raised by 'fungi yeast' is possibly raised by a 'fungible god'. Ironically, the word 'fungible' suggests that Buddhists and Christians may inadvertently and 'interchangeably' be worshipping the same God – which in Christendom is taboo!

7. It is important to note that the poem does NOT assert that the horse and cart analogy is a 'if p therefore q argument' but is merely likened to one.

8. The use of p antecedent and q consequent reminds the poet of 'mind your Ps and Qs'.

Ps and Qs variably stand for 'pints' and 'quarts' and 'pleases' and 'thank yous'.

In a 'discourse', implicitly, one must not get 'drunk' but be fair, objective and polite.

Infinite Universe

In an infinitely large universe
Peopled with hospitable suns
Centillion poets are writing verse!

The law of infinite large numbers runs
Counter to the principle of anarchy
In which my poems are not mine!

By way of an infinite hierarchy
Every verse and every thought
One other poet has uttered ought
Long afore I pen my line!

For in a spinning universe,
Going forward, time goes round;
Regresses till once again, my verse
By and by, comes round and around!

Lawrence Chew
23 Jan 2014

Notes for **Infinite Universe**

In an infinite universe, all that is permitted by the laws of physics will sooner or later happen. But what if the universe is spinning, and spinning with it, time regresses? Mathematicians and physicists have speculated that if one travels at the speed of light along the edge of a spinning universe, it is possible to get back to the starting point before one sets off to go round the universe!

Centillion: 10^{600} (British); 10^{303} (American)

Law of infinite large numbers: large numbers favor the chances of observing an expected event e.g. all things equal, China with its large population will eventually win more Nobel prizes than any other country. An **infinite** large number makes the occurrence inevitable.

Principle of anarchy: this principle asserts any event that is permitted will eventually happen

Infinite hierarchy: an infinite regression of hierarchy that goes back in time

Spinning universe: in a spinning universe, the spinning start and end point is the same point i.e. time has regressed and all that happened has happened before!

Joseph Ponders his Initiation into Adolescence

(PG-rated work of fiction; Pastoral Guidance is advised!)

In a dream of death, desire, guilt and shame,
In body, soul and bed I was mind-spirited
To an undreamt of abode bearing the name
'House of Heaven' as wet tongues of flame

And spurts of hormonal heat coursed red-hot
Through my loins; my eyes wondered among
Temple virgins singing in a strange tongue
In a dance of initiation I understood not

While in my satin skin I lay mind-bound
In a libidinal birth from which I could not wake,
My eyes and ears fixated upon the one sound
I dreaded - an ecstasy of death upon a lake

Of desire! A disrobed virgin strode up to me,
Soothed my nerves and bestrode my groin;
Her belly sought and found my underbelly!
I cried out and felt a rush of flood in my loin.

My affrighted eyes found hers ere she fled,
Fires of desire burning in our ebony-dark eyes!
Bald Potiphar's young, nubile soon-to-wed!
The consummation of dreams I most prize!

Though it is now many years downstream
I still ponder how I may interpret that dream

And wonder how I may sanctify as holy text
That sordid and sodden house of heaven act!

Lawrence Chew
15 Jan 2014

Notes for **Joseph Ponders his Initiation into Adolescence**

Genesis 39 narrates how the adolescent boy slave Joseph resists being seduced by Potiphar's wife but just how true the version is has never being questioned. This poem asks: What if Joseph had succumbed to the seduction? How would he as a prophet of God justify his action?

Mind-spirited: carried away in the spirit (a zeugma as Joseph is spirited away in the body and mind while lying in bed; some critics may think of the sentence structure as a syllepsis)

House of heaven: abode in a temple in which virgins consecrated to deities are kept for ceremonial purposes.

Death: not a physical but spiritual death

Her belly// my underbelly: found my weak spot

Life as an Old Man's Déjà Vu

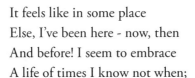

It feels like in some place
Else, I've been here - now, then
And before! I seem to embrace
A life of times I know not when;

The fall of this evening's sunset
Ripens red recesses in the head;
I seem to remember a pale rosette
Of suns in a place of the dead;

I think my gone life is a stream
Of one long fuzzed-out dream,
One half forgotten; the other, ridden
Of all I've been or didn't.

Come, deepening night! While rife
Is life, half-bury my half-lived life
And half-died breaths in meadows
Sun-setting in déjà vu shadows!

Lawrence Chew
30 April 2014

Notes for **Life as an Old Man's Déjà Vu**

A surreal poem in which time and place are fuzzed out like the dreams we have. The dream-like atmosphere is created through the use of run-on lines, alliterations and sibilants.

Alliterations are words beginning with the same letter or sound. Sibilants are words with an s or z sound. In this poem, sibilants are employed to create an atmosphere of sleep and possibly, somnambulism.

Some place/Else: an example of a run-on line employed for the purpose of blurring distinctions of places and time.

Ripens red recesses: an example of alliteration

A pale rosette/of suns: a combination of sibilants and run-on lines to blur distinctions

Fuzzed-out dreams: an example of sibilants

Little Lives in Between Little Deaths

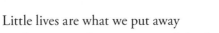

Little lives are what we put away
In closets at night; mementos of the day
Cry out, 'Live us or hie us away!'

Do you not know? Stars and moon sigh
In the wind, 'Unbind us, too soon we die!
We die too much every day!'

Little deaths are what we retrieve
Of closets at dawn; yesterday's brief
Cry out, 'Live us or hive us away!'

Do you not hear? Sun and cloud cry
In the wind, 'Unbind us, too soon we die!
We live too little everyday!'

Unbolt all bars, doors and windows!
Breath of death chills where it blows;
We bind us too much everyday!

Live in the sky, stars, sun and moon;
Live free, live life; we wither too soon;
All bolts, locks and keys throw away.

Lawrence Chew
4 April 2014

Notes for **Little Lives in Between Little Deaths**

This poem is built around two simple activities we subconsciously perform every day – going to bed each night and rising each morning. What is subconscious in these activities is the putting away of our burdens only for us to retrieve them in the morning. All nature cries out to be free – there is no reason why humans should, subconsciously or no, burden themselves.

Closets: cupboards

Mementos: reminders of the past; keepsakes

Hie: hasten

Brief: summary of important matters

Hive: to separate or remove from a group

Lone Sail off Surfers' Paradise. Gold Coast

As
Islets

Cum cloudlets
Tease the eyes, islets
Float by as cloudlets as
Cloudlets drift by as islets
And never the twinned twain
Shall drift alone as two again

But effloresces as one mirage
And one evanescent collage

Drifting out of eye range
That by dint of distance
Deliquesce in grey tint
Beyond which spans
Earth's curvaceous

Expanse -

The white-crested waters of the mighty Pacific
Sleeping out a tumultuous dream
Too dark and deep for words
Too high and wide for birds

Lawrence Chew
26 March 2014

Note for **Lone Sail off Surfers' Paradise, Gold Coast**

Read the 'shape' poem like it is ONE interspersed verse (oxymoron?). Think of the interspersion as a sail painted in bands of different colors but always alternated by the 'blank spacing' of white horizontal stripes. The poetry is as much in the poem's shape and colors as in its wording. Its multicolored shape forms the 'mirage' and 'collage' of a boat with a tiny flag upon a sail rigged to a tall invisible mast. Think of the last verse as the boat's hull plowing through water.

Effloresce: to blossom

Evanesce: to dissipate or disappear as vapor

Deliquesce: to melt away by absorbing moisture from the air

Old-Man-Poet

Old-man-poet! Write from the heart;
Reboot the world; make it new again!
Turn its white hoary head with a start;
Spin a poem of ablative gain!

Let ablution be the God-ablated birth;
Let it unravel the umbilical whorl
That winds a crinkled-wrinkled world
In a fisted babe of death and dearth!

Or die de-poetized! Your dullard eyes
Pluck out or shut! The undead heart lies
Where it bleeds and dies by-the-bye,
Unborn of stars, sun, moon and sky!

Old-man-poet! Shake up, or shut up
The world within your small body of head;
Therein it festers, beaten and drubbed;
Therein with you it dies afore it is dead.

Lawrence Chew
26 March 2014

Notes for **Old-Man-Poet**

A poem of urgency for all who are rapidly aging – and a call to the young to make much of time to live their passion and achieve their dreams! Also, a call to build a new world with God put away.

Reboot: a metaphor from the world of computers, i.e. turn off a computer to get it to start

Turn//start: image in which the world is personified as one who is startled; also, a play on 'reboot' in which one turns off a computer to get it to restart.

Ablative: of excising or cutting away as in ablative surgery

Ablative gain: an oxymoron

Ablution: cleansing, especially as part of a religious rite.

God-ablated birth: a life with God excised

Verse 2: the image employed is that of a caesarian birth

De-poeticized: made unfit for writing poetry

Dullard: (of) dull person

By-the-bye: introducing a new topic

Undead: neither living nor dead; of life without goal, meaning or purpose

Stars, sun, etc: symbols of upper aspirations

Poetry in an Espresso

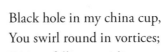

Black hole in my china cup,
You swirl round in vortices;
Rising, falling, twirling up,
You mind me no notices!

In your twirling eye, black
As pitch, I see me in a café;
Sitting up and sitting back,
Stirring black-hole coffee

But my mind too is whirling
In a cupped universe; swirling
Relative to the dark, I go around
Time and come spinning round

One other seminal white hole -
In which my poems swirl up,
Pirouetting toeless as they troll
In a pit holed up in a china cup

Sucking all the I into a vortex
Of nothingness! White hole!
In manifold spirals of the cortex,
Drink me up; spew poems whole!

Lawrence Chew
7 April 2014

Notes for **Poetry in an Espresso**

This poem examines the poet's creative process by comparing the turmoil within him to the imagined turmoil within a black hole. Though no one knows what lies within the infinitely dense void of a black hole, physicists speculate that it has an opposite, a white hole which spews out matter. Some physicists think that a white hole in the past may travel through time to become a black hole in the future. The poet and his readers need not concern themselves about the 'connection' through time. Suffice to say that the connection is an analogy for this poet's creative process.

Black hole: region of space so dense light and matter cannot escape from it

Vortices: swirling mass (of coffee)

Seminal: creative (of seeds or semen; hence a metaphor for being creative)

White hole: hypothetical opposite of a black hole from which matter emerges

Troll: sing

Vortex: a spiral motion that sucks objects into its center.

Manifold//cortex: layered parts or folds of the brain

One-Tree Hill

While I was green and a stripling still,
Machines razed the trees but let one
Stand flag-pole tall in the up-sun
And down-rain atop a denuded hill.

I called the bareness One-Tree Hill,
The tree signposting the way to God
Like Christ upon a cross; near it a rill
White as Christ's blood ran to sod.

I recall a day in my truculent teen
Eagles wheeled over One-Tree Hill;
That day, in the sun-masked sheen,
Splendor bespoke Isaiah 40:31 till

Swooning, one swooping eagle dove
Into that one tree - as in one broken drove
The lesser birds scurried-hurried as one
Thrum of wings into the open net of the sun.

Lawrence Chew
31 March 2104

Notes for **One-Tree Hill**

In this poem the poet recalls the mount upon which Christ was crucified on a 'tree'. The tree is a symbol of the cross- see Galatians 3:13, which read as follows: 'Christ had redeemed us from the curse of the law, being made a curse for us: for it is written, Cursed is everyone that hangeth on a tree.' The poet recalls too the magnificent day he saw eagles wheeling in the sun above the one tree on the hill till one eagle lands on the tree – whereupon all the lesser birds in it took to the open sky in panic there being no other trees around. In an oblique manner of speaking, the poet is questioning whether the tree upon which Christ died offers safety and salvation.

Stripling: an adolescent youth

Truculent: easily annoyed; of a belligerent attitude

Isaiah 40:31: But they that wait upon the Lord shall renew their strength; they shall mount up with wings as eagles; they shall run, and not be weary; and they shall walk, and not faint.

Swooning: in a state of ecstasy

Thrum: dull and monotonous strumming sound (onomatopoeia)

Pondering a Publishing Grant

The terms aren't at all preposterous,
The conditions neither onerous
But still, a leash of the softest strings
Clips bird and song of wings;

My poetry is my constellated moon,
Stars and sun; come bane or boon,
High noon rain or low evening sun
My verse is my daughter and son.

The truth-lipped Muses are undone
When patrilineal gods prostitute
The moon or stars in rain or in sun
And the universe they constitute;

No, I shall not obfuscate or balloon,
Dim or diminish, ever or once,
The coquettish coyness of the moon,
The confabulated boldness of the sun.

Lawrence Chew
11 April 2014

Notes for **Pondering a Publishing Grant**

A publishing grant from a state-run arts council generally comes with terms and conditions. For reasons stated in the poem, this poet did not apply for one.

Preposterous: absurd or ridiculous

Onerous: burdensome or oppressive

Clips: zeugma (figure of speech: a word which applies to two others in different senses)

Wings: also a zeugma (bird and song have 'wings')

Muses: goddesses in Greek mythology, sources of poetic inspiration

Patrilineal: of the father

Obfuscate: to obscure so as to make difficult to perceive or understand

Balloon: to blow up as with a balloon

Coquettish: flirtatious ('coquettish coyness' is an oxymoron)

Confabulated: imagined and fabricated facts that one believes to be true

The Singapore-Schooled Child

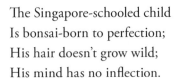

The Singapore-schooled child
Is bonsai-born to perfection;
His hair doesn't grow wild;
His mind has no inflection.

He is just the rare inquiline
His islanded government ordered
For in his rinsed head is recorded
A rhyme: toe the line or pay a fine.

He's a wizard in math and physics
Albeit with no theorem; he critics
The fine arts like the first rate cynics
He admirably mimes and mimics.

He's the perfect bore, spile and pile;
He underpins the bastion of society;
In rank or file, he has no bite, no bile;
The epitome of state-politicized piety!

He'll marry, father bonsai children,
Hold a job and never go on the dole;
Buy and live in a sky-rise warren;
Thank the state for his rabbit hole.

The Singapore child, my perfect child,
He has no genuine guile or venial vile -
For he keeps a straight and public face
That is always within his Stated place.

Bonsai child! Have you no inborn fires?
Be you so correctly prim and trim,
Loosen up, unwind and untwine
Your copper wires!

Promethean child, I haven't a clue
How I may help unbind you;
I am past help, wired too, and bound
In porcelain potted ground.

Lawrence Chew
2 May 2014

Notes: Bonsai is a Japanese art form using miniature trees grown in containers. The limbs of a bonsai plant are trained to stay in their places by winding stiff copper wires around them. In this poem, the bonsai is a metaphor for the child rigidly trained to obey the instructions of those who have authority over him. He is more likely to second guess his superiors and less likely to think for himself. This poem was prompted by two 2014 South Korean incidents: 1. the tragic sinking of the ferry Sewol in which some 200+ students perished because they dutifully followed instructions to remain in their cabins even as the ship was listing and sinking; 2. The collision of two subway trains not many days after the Sewol incident; in this incident, the passengers chose to ignore instructions to remain in their compartments and instead scrambled to safety.

Inflection: a turning or bending away from a course or position of alignment.

Inquiline: an animal that shares its dwelling place with an animal of another species.

Islanded: on an island

Mimes: acts or performs as in a pantomime i.e. without the use of words.

Mimics: imitates closely

Bore: a pun (equipment for boring; one who is tediously uninteresting)

Spile: same meaning as pile

Bastion: part of a defensive stronghold

Bile: bitterness

State-politicized piety: piety promulgated by the state

Epitome: a model for emulation; perfect example

On the dole: living on state welfare

Warren: rabbit hole (metaphor for apartment)

Venial: of sins that are forgivable

Vile: loathsome; disgusting

Stated: a pun (set forth in words; ordered by the state)

Promethean: of Prometheus (see 'A Promethean Poem' on page 34)

Singapore Poet

The poet in cornucopian Singapore
Is an ergonomic misadventure;
He's little less and little more
The definitive backbencher;

He cannot sit easy
At his table or in his chair
Without wondering where
He fits in the economy!

Poet! When asked never say,
'I write poetry,' for vicariously,
Sick mind, sick leave and sick pay
Come to mind invariably;

For the money economy will size
You up with terse empathy in the eye
That mean to say, 'Sorry I asked,
You dumb arse.'

Lawrence Chew
4 May 2014

Notes for **Singapore Poet**

You can't make a living writing poetry (but you can have good times writing poems). In this poem, the economy is personified as a skeptic looking askant on the poet.

Cornucopian: of cornucopia (symbol of prosperity)

Ergonomic: of the applied science of enhancing efficiency and productivity by reducing operator fatigue and discomfort

Misadventure: a mishap or misfortune

Definitive: conclusively agreed upon

Poet!: the poet addresses himself

Backbencher: (a less important) MP who sits at the back (intended as a metaphor)

Vicariously: of taking part in the experience or feelings of another

Invariably: without variation or change

Money economy: economy in which profit is the chief objective

Terse: brief and to the point

Empathy: feeling of deep sympathy

Sleeper in the Casket

The deceased has 2 cusps of lid
Not quite drawn down over the eyes -
I wonder if they are peering askant
Into the afterlife! Pale rouge belies
The flaccid cheeks; pertinaciously hid
The 90+ years he once was ambulant
As rook or bishop on a chessboard
But now light as spirit; stiff as board.

The pate of hair, white among black,
Is slicked down sideways and back;
The trimmed nostril hair knows
Neatness dignifies an upright nose!
But the deep while my heart is cringing,
Mushy mind is surreptitiously thinking,
"O, why does a deceased in repose
Need to look good about the nose?"

I remember an old levitation trick -
Children singing in the thick
Of it:

"Voici un corps mort
Raide comme le marbre
Leger comme spirit
Levi-toi au nom de Jesus Christ!"

I wonder if the quick and the dead
Sleep a walking dream of the head.

15 March 2014
Lawrence Chew

Notes for **Sleeper in the Casket**

A poem on our pre-occupation with vanity in this world and the next.

Pertinaciously: stubbornly or perversely persistent

Ambulant: able to move about freely

Rook: the 'castle' piece in a game of chess

Bishop: another chess piece

Mushy: excessively sentimental

Surreptitiously: secretly

Levitation trick: a children's game, commonly known as 'Light as a feather, stiff as a board' and 'pig in a blanket' (see video clip on YouTube or read Wikipedia for the details of this 'trick' in which children lift a 'sleeper' pretending to be dead, each child employing only 2 fingers of each hand. The game was commonly played when medieval Europe was ravaged by the plague. The 'levitation' symbolized the resurrection of the dead in Christ.

In the thick of it: actively involved in the levitation game

Translation of the 'levitation trick' song:

"Here is a dead body
Stiff as a stick,
Cold as marble,
Light as a spirit
Lift yourself, in Christ's name!"

Putting a Retrocognitive Sci-Fi Spin on Numbers 24:17

(I shall see him, but not now: I shall behold him, but not nigh: there shall come a Star out of Jacob, and a Sceptre shall rise out of Israel, and shall smite the corners of Moab, and destroy all the children of Sheth.)

Ages ago, it began with a bang that started out bad!
In the star-studded swirls of the wispy milky ways,
The prophesied Star of Jacob self-disintegrated
In a nova of cosmic and gamma rays;

We didn't know it then but the implosion razed
And incinerated the planets Moab and Sheth;
All life thereon met (merciful God be praised!)
An instantaneous if horrendous death;

And dying light from the dead star's mayhem
Sped across the vacuous skies of the Milky Way,
Till at long length the magi with exceeding joy
Beheld it as His star over Bethlehem!

Lawrence Chew
27 January 2014

Notes for **Putting a Retrocognitive Sci-Fi Spin on Numbers 24:17**

The poem questions the biblical prophecy that Jesus was the 'Star come out of Jacob'. It questions too whether the star of Bethlehem led the magi to the babe who is to be the Christ. That star is no longer visible today. If that star was a supernova, its death may also mean the total annihilation of one or more populated planets orbiting it and/or other neighboring stars.

Retrocognitive (aka 'postcognitive'): of knowledge of a past event that was not understood at the time it occurred.

Sci-Fi Spin: a science-fiction interpretation (not necessarily scientific or true).

Star of Jacob: the poet imagines that the metaphorical star is a real star which imploded, became a black hole or 'dead star' and hence is no longer visible in the night skies.

Moab and Sheth: ironic names given by the poet to the hapless inhabited planets orbiting the imagined Star of Jacob.

His star: Mathew 2:2: Saying, where is he that is born King of the Jews? For we have seen *his star* in the east, and are come to worship him.

Rolling Trefoil Knot in the Head

(*Interpretaretur sicut vobis placuerit*)

There's a rolling trefoil knot in my head;
It's dormant though it appears to be dead;

It roils my dreams; wakes me when I take
My sleep; sleeps soundly when I wake;

Rolling trefoil knot! What mind are you?
In what contrarian motion do you screw?

I hear you grate and feel your trefoil arc
Pitching and roiling like a question mark.

Dark personified aspects of some godhead!
Dread conscionable thing, non-living undead!

Are you frail spirit of flesh or eternal soul
Or conscionable objector plugging a hole?

How may I break your swirl, twirl and whirl
And not unconscionably roil my inside world?

Christ's unplugged tombstone! Roll you away
I may, you come rolling back some other way.

Lawrence Chew
6 May 2014

Notes for **Rolling Trefoil Knot in the Head**

The poet intends this as a poem left open to interpretations, hence the parenthesis: *Interpretaretur sicut vobis placuerit* (Latin for *Interpret as you please*). The trefoil knot is the symbol for infinity. The reader may like to think of the rolling trefoil knot as symbolizing the conscience or some 'Dark personified aspects' of God, or of both. In the last couplet, the poet likens the knot (i.e. the conscience and dark personified aspects of God) to the stone placed at the entrance to Christ's tomb. As with the trefoil knot rolling in the poet's head, the reader has to decide what the rolled-away tombstone symbolizes: is the poet merely talking about one's conscience or the conscience as some troubling 'personified aspects' of a 'dark' God?

The trefoil knot is a loop formed by joining together the two loose ends of a common overhand knot. It is the simplest example of a non-trivial knot i.e. you cannot 'untie' it in 3 dimensions without cutting it (see my poem 'A Dream of Being in a Trefoil Tunnel' on page 22).

Smug Dreamers

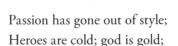

Passion has gone out of style;
Heroes are cold; god is gold;
Virtue is vile.

The times have made us soft,
Stole us our hunger and thunder
And sold us the floor for the loft;

The divine fire Prometheus lit
In the heart glows slow and low
It smolders so in its cold pit.

Achilles and Patroclus die unborn,
Hector cowers in fear; Shakespeare's
At the movies smooching pop corn;

The poetry of earth bleeds red;
Keats' in the womb; Yeats' in the tomb;
The Pierian fountain dries at its head.

Beneath the dome-vaulted skies
We sleep-walk and sleep-talk
The unborn dead into our lives;

The unborn dead sleep in us!
Death convalesces in the head
In conurbation of muck and pus.

Lawrence Chew
9 April 2014

Notes for **Smug Dreamer**

In an age of plenty, smug complacency is a threat to the wellbeing of mankind. We become less inclined to achieve for the wellbeing of all.

Smug: self-satisfied, complacent

Verse 1: inversion of socially accepted values

Stole: a zeugma (figure of speech; a word that applies to two others in different senses)

Prometheus: Titan who stole and taught men how to use fire.

Achilles: Greek hero in the Iliad

Patroclus: Achilles' beloved comrade and brother in arms

Hector: noble Trojan hero who killed Patroclus and whose death Achilles avenged

Shakespeare: world's greatest playwright

Keats: Romantic poet (1795 – 1821) best known for 'Ode to a Nightingale'

Yeats: Irish Nobel Prize poet (1865 – 1939)

Poetry of earth: allusion to Keats' opening line in 'On the Grasshopper and Cricket'

Pierian fountain: a spring sacred to the Muses

Dome-vaulted skies: allusion to a crypt or necropolis

Death convalesces: personification of death as a patient recovering from an illness

Conurbation: large expansion of cities over wider areas

Muck: dirt, rubbish, waste matter

If You're Thinking of Going Up to Heaven

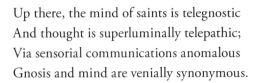

Up there, the mind of saints is telegnostic
And thought is superluminally telepathic;
Via sensorial communications anomalous
Gnosis and mind are venially synonymous.

All is public fare; the personal life is dead
And every thought you surfed in your head
Is served on www@heaven.com at the click
Of some button of a mouse or joy-stick!

Heaven! Wikipedia@heaven.com is up there
And good by jolly golly, beware, beware!
You have better not be up to nothing sorry
For WikiLeaks@heaven.com has your story!

Every angel is a JulianAssange whistleblower
And every sexless saint a BradleyManning -
For BradleyManning is a.k.a. Chelsea manning
Tattletale@heaven.com or some.com other!

And in the Lord's secret service, every agent
Is a self-appointed Edward Joseph Snowden
Who will convince you his service is cogent;
When he warms up to you he means to cozen!

And hell! There's always Twitter or Facebook
Whereat Popes and Holy Inquisitors may look
Into every cranny, every hole and every nook
When you thumb God a nose or cock a snook!

Listen up good! God's heaven is a glass-house
Wherein no saint is a trysting lover or spouse;
All privies to secrets are naked in the main -
Downloadable as porn in the public domain!

So if you're thinking of going up to heaven,
You mightn't want to live it up in the blue
If you know telegnosis is the yeast that leaven
The mushy mind into a dipsomaniac brew!

Lawrence Chew
16 February 2014

Notes for **If You're Thinking of Going Up to Heaven**

This whimsical poem pokes fun at what it's like in a fully transparent heaven. The theist is brought up to believe heaven is a place of eternal bliss. This poet begs to differ!

Telegnostic: of knowledge obtained without the use of normal sensory means

Sensorial communication anomalous: communication by extrasensory or paranormal means

Gnosis: knowledge (including knowledge gained from spiritual or mystical sources)

Venially synonymous: can be forgiven for thinking that mind and gnosis are one and the same (venially = pardonably)

The personal life is dead: line from Boris Pasternak's novel 'Doctor Zhivago'

Julian Assange: name of equally-loved and hated (?) international whistleblower

Bradley Manning: transgender whistleblower who changed his name to Chelsea Manning

Surfed and served: puns

Manning and manning: puns

Privies: participants in knowledge of something private, secret or classified

Dipsomaniac: (of) an insatiable craving for alcoholic beverages

The Gone Years Versified as a Poem

This much I fretfully remember of what I've fitfully forgotten:
While yesterdays die immortalized and tomorrows lie unbegotten-
The chrysanthemum-bursts of sun-roused morns in the early east;
The moony shades of dew-doused dusks - and of late but not least,
While I poeticize the dreams of songs tripping off the tongue,
Time, unbeknown, transfigures me old ere my lines are done.

Like to the dimwitted stars sleep-telling little ones mortal stories,
Like to the passing clouds jointly-and-severally dismembered
In showers of dissolution, the gone years precipitate memories
Of fatefully begotten poetry fretfully lost and fitfully forgotten
But now, then and again, roundly and redundantly remembered.

Lawrence Chew
28 June 2013

Notes for The Gone Years Versified as a Poem

The poet thinks of his gone years as a poem he wrote and which he can now hardly recall! The poem further suggests that the older the poet gets the more shadowy and ambivalent is the nostalgia he experiences. Remembering is as difficult as forgetting a poem because all about the aging poet, everything is heading towards the precipice of dissolution. Still, one has to be thankful for the times good or bad. Alliteration abounds in his poem – the poet intends these as symbolic of his struggle to recall and remember his gone years. This poem is dedicated to a fan CCL - who adores the images in this and many other of his poems.

Fretfully: of an inclination to be troubled or vexed

Fitfully: occurring in intermittent bursts

Immortalized: remembered as something eternal

Unbegotten: not yet born

Chrysanthemum-burst: sunrise remembered as a chrysanthemum in bloom

Early east: symbolic of early years

Verse 2: the poet compares himself to sleepy stars that tell forgotten stories and to 'showers of dissolution'. The stars and showers are images of forgetfulness and dissolution. The phrase 'jointly-and-severally' is an oxymoronic phrase borrowed term from legal parlance.

Roundly: with force or vigor

Redundantly: unnecessarily

To Orioles Flit-Flirting in the Sun

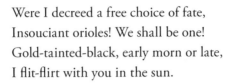

Were I decreed a free choice of fate,
Insouciant orioles! We shall be one!
Gold-tainted-black, early morn or late,
I flit-flirt with you in the sun.

No gravity of custom flags me down
No laws forbid me to fly, flit or flirt
My heart is my soul; my head my crown;
My wings abhor human dirt.

No kings lord over me but the sun
No queens look askant but the moon,
No gods forge me since time begun
The embryonic egg that hatch a zoon.

I rise to my height; no winds fetter;
No out-of-bound markers letter
Where I nest, banish where I go –
I am my god that makes me so.

I shall never sing in a netted cage;
Death knows not the pain of chain.
In infrangible sun, moon and rain
I fly; freedom my wager and wage.

Lawrence Chew
30 April 2014

Notes for **To Orioles Flit-Flirting in the Sun**

The black nape orioles are incredibly playful birds – for this reason, they are this poet's favorite bird for they symbolize all that is free and untainted notwithstanding that their nape is 'tainted' with black.

Insouciant: free from anxiety and worries

Gold-tainted-black: the colors of the black nape oriole

Flit-flirt: paired orioles commonly flirt in playful flight

Gravity: seriousness, an intended pun – gravity as a force pulls one down

Flags: to weigh or pull down

Abhor: hate; loathe

Height: symbol of fulfillment

Zoon: an animal developed from a fertilized egg

Out-of-bound markers: markers placed on a golf course

Infrangible: unbreakable; incapable of being broken

The Ten Commandments of Truth

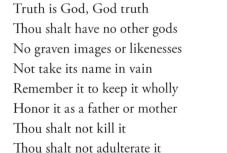

Truth is God, God truth
Thou shalt have no other gods
No graven images or likenesses
Not take its name in vain
Remember it to keep it wholly
Honor it as a father or mother
Thou shalt not kill it
Thou shalt not adulterate it
Thou shall seal it
Thou shalt not bear false witness to it
Thou shall covet it.

Lawrence Chew
6 April 2014

Notes for **The Ten Commandments of Truth**

This poem needs little explanation. Suffice to say, it is a parody of the Ten Commandments as paraphrased on Wikipedia.

Graven: made as carvings, sculptures

Wholly: completely

Adulterate: dilute

Seal: to establish or affirm

Covet: to lust after

Vox Populi Vox Dei

Mobs through the roiling ages
Cry, 'Vox populi vox dei'
That for better or worse, weigh
Hard on history's insensate pages;

Socrates was popularly urged
To consume hemlock:
The Athenian mob mocked
And had the gadfly purged;

'Crucify him', with one voice
The Jews of Jerusalem cried;
Pilate had little choice
And so Jesus died;

Peasants, proletariats stormed
Palaces; wise, heretics beheaded;
No *populi* was more dreaded
No *vox* louder than the ill-informed;

Nations still go to war
Little knowing what for;
Revolutionaries are born
And hanged afore morn.

Guillotines and hangmen
Silhouette and adorn
The false dawn
Of tyrants' enlightenment;

Revolutions devour
The babes they give birth to;
Tyrants, despots, popes too
Overstay their hour.

'Vox populi vox dei'
But few question why they
Raged, killed, burnt and fought
Or thought to ask God what He thought.

Lawrence Chew
15 April 2014

Notes for **Vox Populi Vox Dei**

The clamor 'Vox populi vox Dei' predates the days of the Eastern Roman Empire. It means in Latin 'the voice of the people is the voice of God'. The poet thinks it strange that the people who use (more likely abuse) this old proverb never think it strange not to ask God what he thinks! The tone of the poem is one of sarcasm.

Roiling ages: of the troubled ages

Insensate: lacking physical sensation

Proletariat: wage earners

Populi: Latin for 'people'

Vox: Latin for 'voice'

Silhouette: dark outline of a person, object

Adorn: decorate

World at my Window

World at my window, my window-framed world!
You twist and twirl my giddy-headed breath awhirl!
In sun and moon and rain you look in and walk on by;
In shade and dew-fall and wind, you heed not my sigh.
In my three-score years of commingled joys and cares
You scorn and laugh off my worry-come and sorry-go
And I, still the wild-eyed child dreaming his nightmares,
Know not I why like you I scurry-hurry-go to and fro
Yet cannot tell from whence meaning draws its breath,
The nights and days I live and die my years of death.

World at my window, my window-world! You swirl,
Twist, twirl, rock and roil my hair-thin head awhirl!
Come tomorrow, some other soul in my vacated chair
Shall draw for breath my expired, giddy-headed air!

Lawrence Chew
23 Oct 2013

Notes for **World at my Window**

This poem is a portrait of what the world looks like through the eyes of a child to the day he grows old and dies. The portrait is alluded to in the phrase 'my window-framed world'. As the world turns and the child grows old, the poem comes full circle: another child will take the old man's vacated chair and breathe in the giddy-headed air he expired. Throughout the poem, it remains unclear if the persona will discover any meaning in life. Alliterations and rhymes help to reinforce the impression of a giddy-headed world intoxicated by the beautiful and the sublime with all its pains and angst.

World at my window: the poet addresses a personified world

Commingled: mixed, blended

Vacated: left as unoccupied

Vivovdan. 28 June 1914

Sarajevo's veneer of calm that Vivovdan
Belies the state of hate in the natural man;
For man, bungling in his invidious state,
Is bumbling friend and foe of dicey Fate;

That uneasy morn, before holy St. Vitus,
Six irredentists of the infamous Black Hand
Swore and eulogized with wine and victus,
The suicide vows of Vivovdan.

To free all Serbs of foreign tyranny,
They spaced and lined along Appel Quay,
Each praying God grant the martyrdom
Of Archduke Franz Ferdinand!

As flip-flop Fate would want it to happen,
And the slip-shod hands of God sloven,
No plans followed their planned sequences;
All Europe would suffer the consequences!

One bomb missed; the Duke got away
But not so the many harm put in the way;
Shaken but relieved, Ferdinand figured
It wouldn't do harm to visit the injured.

The car turned up a wrong road;
It reversed but Fate made a no-go of it;
Its gears locked and God could not goad
The car pass Moritz Schiller's one bit.

At the café's alfresco on a fluke,
Black Hand Princip saw the Duke!
Inadvertence works better than charm;
He welcomed the Duke with firearm!

Roundly, the two bullets he fired
Found the Royals he so jurally desired!
And so, that Vivovdan of 1910 and four,
All Europe heard rumblings of war!

The war brought all Europe to a boil
Hot as St. Vitus' pot of bubbling oil!
Churches on either side the divide
Prayed God sow death on the other side!

God heard the prayers and wondered
How best to answer either side equitably well;
He slept three whole years as He pondered
What plague might make war a hotter hell!

Sixteen million died in the Great War!
Of influenza add fifty million or more!
God of St. Vitus! St. Vitus of God,
Is man God's detritus, good only as sod?

Though I wasn't born then,
It sickens me to no end
To think Fate's chastening rod
Is mightier than crook of God

So angst-stricken was I
I gave up being God's trembling theist
And swore to absentee God in the sky

I shall hence be a born-again atheist!

I take sole sovereignty of my soul
If soul-in-body I have any;
Let the finite be my only goal
And the infinite be for astronomy.

But oh, shut up, gape-open Mouth!
I glory not in being my irredentist -
Which is little better, I vouch,
Than being my own dentist.

Lawrence Chew
29 January 2014

Notes on **Vivovdan 28 June 1914**

This poem is written to mark the 100th anniversary of World War 1.

Vivovdan: a festival marking the martyrdom of St Vitus and all Slavs who gave their lives fending off the Ottoman Empire's domination of Serbia (homeland of the Slavs and Serbs).

Sarajevo: Serbian capital city in which Duke Franz Ferdinand (heir-apparent to the throne of the Austrian-Hungarian Empire) was assassinated. The assassination precipitated the First World War.

Black Hand: band of Serb irredentists who were determined to free Serbia of the Austrian-Hungarian Empire.

St. Vitus: a Christian martyr; he was boiled to death.

Irredentists: nationalists who seek to recover lost territories.

(Gavrilo) Princip: the Black Hand member who assassinated Duke Ferdinand and his Duchess.

Moritz Schiller's Café: the assassination took place near this café.

Somewhere, Somewhen

Somewhere at all moments,
A new sun is rising
As half a good earth away,
The old is setting.

Somewhere at all moments,
Bright day is breaking
As half a black sky away,
Dark night is falling.

Somewhere at all moments,
Midday is waking
As half a diurnal day away,
Midnight is sleeping.

And somewhere at all moments,
A newborn babe is crying
As somewhere else that moment,
Some babe's mother is dying.

Rising, setting, breaking, falling,
Waking, sleeping, crying, dying -
Somewhere, somewhen, at all moments,
Dreams and miracles come together,

Entropically, fall apart together.

Lawrence Chew
26 February 2014

Notes for **Somewhere, Somewhen**

At all moments of the day and night, day breaks and night falls somewhere on the earth as it rotates. In between, midday and midnight routinely occur. We think of these wondrous happenings as dreams and miracles that come together and often, it is only when we are struck by some tragedy that we realize that dreams and miracles are part and parcel of the entropy process in which all things come together only to fall apart. Though unstated, implicit in this poem is the poet's atheistic belief that human beings do not have any 'special' or 'starring role' in the cosmic drama around us. From an impersonal point of view, our coming and going, are parts of the dynamic process known as entropy.

Diurnal: relating to or occurring in a 24-hour period; daily

Entropically: of entropy, the inevitable and steady deterioration of a system or society.

Angst of an Old Walking-Dead

If I were again a stripling lad today
I shall put all gods and devils away;
I know what sins I shall not have to pay!

I am rag-and-bone-tired of playing dead
And of acquiring a required pig's head
Not mine but some governing swine;

Out! Bounds and barbs that augment
Subordination! Gods, bibles and churches;
Education, state and government -

You that fart jingoes on high perches
And lobotomize the tongue of the young;
All you mindbenders,

Bugger off! I'm no head of lead!
Go opiate your own godhead;
I am not your walking dead.

I am my sum and totality
The aggregate entity in my identity;
I'll not be deliquesced into anonymity!

My head should get along fine
If you mind your part of sky and I,
Where I breathe, mind mine!

Lawrence Chew
17 May 2014

Notes for **Angst of an Old Walking-Dead**

The angst in this poem is directed at establishments that throughout history are thought to be ultimate sources of authority and morality.

Sins: permissible acts (as opposed to criminal acts)

Rag-and-bone tired: metaphor for impoverishment of spirit, of being given discards

Jingoes: patriotic, chauvinistic or moralized exhortations

Lobotomize: to deprive of energy and vitality (also, a term from brain surgery)

Mind-benders: those who dull the mind

Opiate: to dull the mind

Aggregate entity in my identity: oxymoron and pun; parts amounting to a whole

Deliquesced: be melted away by absorbing moisture from the air

Part of sky: personal symbol for one's breathing space and dreams

The City as a Tableau Vivant of Anonymity and Dissolution

In the late after-set of the sun
Busloads, one by every one,
Take their leave; so soul-bereft,
The city acquiesces to its death.

Above ground, slowly drive
Or under, lumber where you will -
In its halogen-shriven world,
The necropolis comes alive;

Orangey orbits and elliptical fuzz
Of halogen lamps bathe and buzz
The streets, as reminiscent of Hades,
My silhouette fades into shades.

Like you, Hades-benighted city,
My halogen twilight deepens;
As its dark dissolution steepens,
I too deliquesce into anonymity.

Lawrence Chew
16 May 2014

Notes for The City as a Tableau Vivant of Anonymity and Dissolution

Dreams, anonymity and dissolution are recurring themes in this poet's work. In this poem, the city, as is the poet in his twilight years, is a 'tableau vivant' of life and death.

By day, the city is vibrant and alive but as night approaches, emptied of souls, it 'acquiesces to its death'. In like manner, the poet in his twilight years deliquesces into anonymity.

Tableau vivant: living picture or portrait (French)

Acquiesces: consent passively to

Halogen-shriven: washed in halogen light

Necropolis: city of the dead; cemetery

Orangey orbits // fuzz: shape and color cast by light from street lamps

Hades: abode of the dead (Greek mythology)

Silhouette: dark outline of the poet

Deliquesce: melt or dissolve by absorbing moisture from the air

You Dreamed Me

While I was not yet awake or dead
You dreamed me in your dark head;
People! Me, you invoked and evoked
So out of my anonymity, I awoke;

You uttered my ineffable name,
So I rose from my slumber and became
Ensconced in your minds as ineluctable,
Ineffaceable, inenarrable, and inerrable!

I shall lead you, to and fro, into dreams
Illuminant as the high-spirited streams
Of an upper consciousness scrolled away
In superlunary spirals of the Milky Way!

I, your God, command you, one and all:
Evoke me; invoke me; uplift me, and fall
As one upon hands and knees; so only I
Rise, as all you fall, in one blink of an eye.

Lawrence Chew
18 March 2014

Notes for **You Dreamed Me**

The persona in the poem is the voice of God. God tells how He came to be created. The choice of bombastic words in verse 2 is meant as an irony! The people who dreamed up an all wise and omniscient God created Him in their heads but may not know the meanings of the words the God they created know!

Evoked: summoned or called forth.

Invoked: called upon a higher power for assistance, help, etc.

Conjured: summoned (a spirit) by magic, invocation, etc.

Ineffable name: a name that is incapable of being uttered.

Ineluctable: not to be avoided or escaped, inevitable.

Ensconced: settled or established firmly.

Ineffaceable: indelible; cannot be erased.

Inerrable: incapable of erring; infallible.

Inenarrable: incapable of being narrated or told.

Illuminant: giving off much light.

Superlunary: above the moon.

Fall: double entendre (fall down as in worship, fall as in a failing)

Holiness

(For Bruno Giordano)

Holiness, Giordano, is a tumor
That first presents as benign;
I say not in wry humor but honor
It may the soul malign.

Every now, so and then
The benign becomes a danger
As every now, so and when
A tumor becomes a cancer.

O what gall of stone it must take
To assert a tumor was born to save
You, cancer exciser, from your grave:
Burning you Giordano at the stake!

Archetypal Christ-child,
You were born benign and mild
But the holier you mean us to be,
Likelier, the more cancerous we!

Lawrence Chew
29 May 2014

Notes for **Holiness**

The poem is presented as a personal address to Bruno Giordano (1548–1600), a Dominican friar, philosopher, mathematician, scientist and poet. He was burned at the stake in Rome for advocating a heliocentric solar system and a universe of stars possibly populated by inhabited planets. Given below are 2 of his utterances that damned him.

"In space there are countless constellations, suns and planets; we see only the suns because they give light; the planets remain invisible, for they are small and dark. There are also numberless earths circling around their suns..."

"Unless you make yourself equal to God, you cannot understand God: for the like is not intelligible save to the like. Make yourself grow to greatness beyond measure, by a bound free yourself from the body; raise yourself above all time, become Eternity; then you will understand God. Believe that nothing is impossible for you, think yourself immortal and capable of understanding all, all arts, all sciences, the nature of every living being. Mount higher than the highest height; descend lower than the lowest depth. Draw into yourself all sensations of everything created, fire and water, dry and moist, imagining that you are everywhere, on earth, in the sea, in the sky, that you are not yet born, in the maternal womb, adolescent, old, dead, beyond death. If you embrace in your thought all things at once, times, places, substances, qualities, quantities, you may understand God."

Tumor: abnormal growth of tissue resulting from uncontrolled, progressive multiplication of cells and serving no physiological function; a neoplasm

Present: manifest as a part of a disease or medical condition

Benign: of no danger to health

Malign: cause harm

A Quick Prayer, if Wishy-washy, to Myself

Grant me but these easy wishes:
Simple fare my daily dishes;
Safe fare from vice and vanity;
Work-joy, love, peace and sanity;
A quiet mind and quiet breath
And when I die, a quiet death;

Thereafter, grant me dissolution,
Anonymity and sweet oblivion
So I need no telegnostic heaven
Nor fear hell but etherized of evil,
Be amortized of God and devil.

And if these be wishy-washy wishes
Or to God and devil diabolical dishes,
Nor move Neither to do good but evil,
How is God different from the devil?

O, Sins that live forever! how sad!
If God like Satan is never any good
For it would seem, or one may deem,

God is Satan in a good mood,
Satan is God in a bad.

Lawrence Chew
14 Oct 2013

Fare: a pun on 'fare' as food and journey

Dissolution: decomposition

Anonymity: state of being unknown

Oblivion: state of being completely forgotten

Telegnostic: of knowledge obtained through extra-sensory means

Etherized: be anaesthetized

Amortized: of debts gradually written off over a period

Acknowledgement

The author would like to thank:

Jeffery Lee for writing the Foreword;

Shelly Edmunds, Publishing Service Associate at Partridge Singapore for her patience and encouragement (she has a sweet nature!);

Christian Jay, Senior Publishing Consultant at Partridge Singapore for his advice and encouragement.